Chasing Charles
by:
JJ Buechner

CHASING CHARLES
Copyright © 2015, JJ Buechner
CAUTION: Professional and amateurs are hereby warned that performances of CHASING CHARLES are subject to payment of royalty. It is fully protected under the copyright laws of the United States of America and all of the countries covered by the International Copyright Union (including the Dominion of Canada and the rest of the British Commonwealth). The English language stock and amateur stage performance rights in the United States, its territories, possessions, and Canada for CHASING CHARLES are controlled exclusively by the playwright JJ Buechner, localactorsguild@gmail.com. No professional or nonprofessional performances of the play may be given without obtaining in advance the written permission of playwright JJ Buechner and paying the requisite fee.

Characters

CHARLES - Makeup & Wig Designer. 30's, Italian and charming.

DENNIS - Charles' best friend and business partner, 30's.

ANGELA - Charles' overbearing Italian Mother, 50's.

EDWARD - Wig designer. Flamboyant, witty, and funny. 30's40's

BRIAN - A hustler who later becomes Charles' boyfriend. 20's

CAROL - An Opera soprano – 20's-30's

RICHARD - An Opera baritone – 20's-30's. Also plays the Male Nurse

From the playwright – these characters are real people and should be played as such, if you are genuine the comedy will shine through the drama.

Chasing Charles premiered as part of The New Play Festival at The Local Actors Guild of Saratoga, December 13th, 2014. It was directed by Hollie Miller, costume & wig design by Edna Capri, sound design by JJ Buechner. The production was stage managed by Steve Moulton who also designed the lighting. The cast was as follows:

Charles - Matt Demarco
Dennis - JJ Buechner
Angela - Ann Milliken
Edward - Oliver Ord
Brian - Nathan Hoffmann
Carol - Elizabeth Sterling
Richard/Male Nurse - Chad Radock

Chasing Charles had a fully staged production with The Local Actors Guild of Saratoga that opened November 14th, 2015. It was directed by Jonathan Pate, costume & wig design by Edna Capri, sound design by JJ Buechner. The production was stage managed by Steve Moulton who also designed the lighting. Nick Himmelwright was Assistant Stage Manager. The cast was as follows:

Charles - Matt Demarco
Dennis - JJ Buechner
Angela - Ann Milliken and Melissa Putterman-Hoffmann
Edward - Oliver Ord
Brian - Christopher Malatesta
Carol - Elizabeth Sterling
Richard/Male Nurse - Chad Radock

Act One

Scene 1 - San Diego 1974, Fall. Dennis' Apartment.
Scene 2 - NYC. Spring, 1976. Split Scene. The Wig Studio/Charles Bedroom.
Scene 3 - New Orleans. Fall, 1978. Backstage, the New Orleans Opera. Final dress for Massenet's "Thais."
Scene 4 - NYC. Spring, 1979. Backstage at the Metropolitan Opera. Opening night of "La Boheme."

Act Two

Scene 1 - NYC. July 3, 1981. The Wig Studio.
Scene 2 - NYC. Fall, 1984. Split Scene. Wig Studio/Charles Apartment.
Scene 3 - May 1985. Charles' Hospital Room. St Vincent's Hospital.
Scene 4 - NYC. May 28, 1985. Split Scene. Wig Studio/Charles' Hospital Room.
Scene 5 - The Next Morning. Charles' Bedroom.

A note about the music

Each scene change should have music. It should reflect the time period and the scene of the play. Some music is noted in the stage directions.

It is also very important to not have scene change music between Act 2, Scene 4 & Act 2, Scene

Charles R. Elsen, studied singing as a tenor at the Juilliard School of Music. He entered the New York City Opera cloister in 1967, and while there, was encouraged by Beverly Sills, Julius Rudel and Tito Capobianco to pursue a career as a makeup artist. He established Charles Elsen & Associates to collaborate on makeup and wig design with companies throughout America and abroad in consultation with directors and designers. Among companies with which Mr. Elsen worked were the New York City Opera, the Washington Opera, the Cincinnati Opera, the Edinburgh Festival and the Australian Opera in Sydney. He also created individualized makeup and wigs for singers including Miss Sills, Joan Sutherland, Birgit Nilsson, Placido Domingo, Luciano Pavarotti, Richard Tucker and Victoria de Los Angeles. The well-remembered makeup worn by Norman Treigle and Samuel Ramey as the devil in "Mefistofele" was Mr. Elsen's creation. Mr. Elsen's work was seen on many installments of the PBS Great Performances series, on "Live from the White House" and on several other programs. Mr. Elsen was responsible for the wig and make up design for the 1983 Broadway revival of "On Your Toes,", starring Natalia Makarova, and the 1981 off-Broadway production of *Miss Julie* for the Roundabout Theatre Company.

Act 1

Scene 1

(Scene opens with Charles sitting on the bed in his boxer shorts. There is a small box of Fiestaware on the floor at the foot of the bed. There is also a small bag of beauty supplies on the nightstand. Charles notices a curling iron sticking out of a beauty supply bag. Charles is looking through the box of Fiestaware as Dennis enters wearing a bathrobe.)

DENNIS: Hey.
CHARLES: Hey. What's all this stuff?
DENNIS: It's called Fiestaware.
CHARLES: Fiestaware?
DENNIS: Yeah, it's vintage plates and cups. Mostly from the 1930's. I know they're kind of old fashioned, but I love the bright colors.
CHARLES: They're definitely bright.
DENNIS: Yeah, they are.
CHARLES: This is a really cool apartment. It reminds me of home.
DENNIS: You grew up in a Victorian house?
CHARLES: No, I grew up in a little one family in the suburbs, but the city I lived in had a lot of the same type of homes.
DENNIS: Wow, you really don't look like the suburban type. You look more like a city boy.
CHARLES: I haven't been called a boy in a long time. I grew up close to a city called Schenectady. Have you ever heard of it?
DENNIS: No, I haven't.

13

CHARLES: It's a pretty big city. General Electric started there. It's mostly Italian.
DENNIS: It sounds like it was a great place to grow up.
CHARLES: Not for a young gay kid like me. Don't get me wrong it was okay, but I knew I wanted more so I moved to Manhattan when I was sixteen to study opera at the Julliard School.
DENNIS: All by yourself at sixteen? Your parents just let you go?
CHARLES: I think they knew upstate wasn't really my scene. Besides I wasn't by myself. My parents made one of my cousins go with me. They wanted him to keep an eye on me, ya know, just to make sure I didn't go wild. *(Laughs to himself.)* If they only knew.
DENNIS: I'm guessing there was no way taming you.
CHARLES: I had my fun, but I wanted to do opera so bad that I wasn't going to let anything get in my way of becoming a star.
DENNIS: A star?
CHARLES: I wish. It was always my dream to go to Julliard and become a lead opera tenor, but I ended up in the cloister. Which I found out wasn't such a bad gig. I got a job in at City Opera in Manhattan. I traveled everywhere and I got to work with great artists. Then I met Beverly Sills and my life changed.
DENNIS: Who's Beverly Sills?
CHARLES: She's a famous Soprano, her voice is amazing. She mostly went by her nickname "Bubbles."

DENNIS: Bubbles?
CHARLES: She won a Beautiful Baby contest when she was a child and was billed as "Bubbles" Silverman. *(They both share a laugh.)* Anyway, I always had a knack for doing makeup and she liked the way I did my own face, so she asked me to do hers a couple times. Then she tells her friends about me and the next thing you know I'm the go to guy for opera makeup. That's why I'm starting my own makeup and wig company in New York City.
DENNIS: What are you doing in California?
CHARLES: I'm here doing makeup at San Diego Opera. But to be quite honest that's not the only reason I'm here. Max Factor does all the wigs for MGM and they are getting out of the business. So, I'm buying their entire wig collection.
DENNIS: That must be costing you a pretty penny.
CHARLES: Not me. I have investors. A wealthy couple from Chicago believes in my talent and feels I should take a chance. *(A little laugh from Dennis.)* I guess you can say I'm pretty charming.
DENNIS: I'd have to agree. Do you always just meet men on the street and "charm" them up to their apartments?
CHARLES: I wouldn't call what I did charming you. I had to chase you a little. You did duck into that bookstore.
DENNIS: I don't usually get picked up on the street like that.
CHARLES: You almost lost me in the non-fiction section, but I like the chase. I had to chase my boyfriend too, but I caught him.
DENNIS: Your boyfriend?

CHARLES: Does that bother you? *(No response.)* We have an agreement. I agree not to tell him anything and he never questions me.
DENNIS: That's very 70's of you.
CHARLES: I like that. It is a very 70's thing. It's more of a Manhattan thing.
DENNIS: I wouldn't know. I've never been to Manhattan.

(Dennis starts to get dressed.)

CHARLES: It's the most amazing place; the whole city is like one big pick-up scene, bathhouses, and backrooms. The coolest place is a section of Central Park called the Rambles, it's like there's a man behind every tree just waiting to play.
DENNIS: Sounds a little different from where you grew up, huh?
CHARLES: So different. It's like…I didn't know what it was like to live until I got there. The whole city just has this vibe that I can't explain. You're going to love it there.
DENNIS: I'm sure if I ever visit I will.
CHARLES: Why not now?
DENNIS: What are you talking about?
CHARLES: Look, I'm an amazing makeup artist but I can't style wigs to save my life. I already have one wig stylist named Edward, but I could use someone like you.
DENNIS: I don't know how to style wigs.

(Charles grabs a curling iron out of the hairstyling bag on the nightstand and waves it in Dennis' face.)

16

CHARLES: Really? Well, this begs to differ.

(Dennis grabs the curling iron away from Charles.)

DENNIS: I cut and style hair.
CHARLES: That's perfect. I can design the style. You can set it and style it. It's just like doing hair.
DENNIS: But I don't know anything about wigs, and I hate Opera. All that crazy high-pitched singing in Italian, I can't even understand what the hell they're saying. *(Charles starts laughing.)* What are you laughing at?
CHARLES: You are very cute when you ramble.
DENNIS: Listen, I just met you. We shared a very nice afternoon together but that's it. I'm very happy here. *(Charles starts laughing again.)* Stop laughing at me.

(Dennis picks up Charles' clothes and throws them at him.)

(Continued) Here…take your clothes, your 70's Manhattan charm and leave.
CHARLES: Okay. I just thought I'd show you what it was like to live.
DENNIS: Excuse me? You don't even know me. I live a lot.
CHARLES: Oh really? How many men have you slept with?
DENNIS: I really don't think that's any of your business.

CHARLES: Have you ever been to a bathhouse? A backroom? *(No response from Dennis.)* I didn't think so.
DENNIS: Just leave.

(Charles starts to get dressed.)

CHARLES: Fine. If you want to stay in California setting old ladies' hair every Friday that's fine by me, but you could have more.
DENNIS: I don't want to become someone in your man stable. *(Charles laughs again.)* You really are irritating you know that?
CHARLES: I thought I was charming.
DENNIS: You were charming. *(Change of tone.)* Look, it seems like a great offer, but I don't know you and you don't know me. I could be a murderer.
CHARLES: You are not a murderer. Not with that innocent face.
DENNIS: Ya know, not every gay man wants to live in New York City. Did you even stop and look around to see how beautiful San Diego is? Maybe if you looked past the manhunt you'd see it differently.
CHARLES: I see what I want to see. I'm not blind to beauty. Don't forget I'm an artist.
DENNIS: Oh, please you do makeup I wouldn't call that art.
CHARLES: Really?

(Charles goes to his bag, he takes out a photo album of his work and throws it on the bed.)

DENNIS: What's this?
CHARLES: Open it.

(Dennis sits on the bed and opens the album. He starts looking over the photos.)

DENNIS: You did these Charles?
CHARLES: Yes.
DENNIS: These are really beautiful. Who's this?
CHARLES: That's Samuel Ramey as the devil in "Mefistofele" from the Opera Faust. It's my favorite makeup. It was the first makeup design that was my full creation. That was the moment I knew I wanted to start my own company.
DENNIS: Who taught you how to do this?
CHARLES: I taught myself. When I was a kid I did a lot of singing in choirs, that's when I fell in love with opera. I started buying as many records as I could, and I studied the pictures on the inside. I used-to make myself up in the bathroom. After a while I wanted to make-up other people so I would invite my aunts and uncles over. I'd assign them parts in operas. Then I would make up their faces to look like the characters and direct them.

(Dennis turns the page in the book.)

(Continued) And that's me working on Beverly Sills.

DENNIS: She's beautiful. These are really amazing. *(Small pause.)* I'm sorry I said you weren't an artist. I should have known when I saw your hands.

19

CHARLES: My hands?
DENNIS: You have the hands of an artist.
CHARLES: No way, I have the hands of an Italian peasant.

(Dennis picks up a loose photo that fell out of the book when he opened it.)

DENNIS: Who's this?
CHARLES: That's me performing in the ensemble of "The Pirates of Penzance."
DENNIS: You look very handsome in this picture.

(Looks at Charles, notices he is blushing.)

(Continued) Are you blushing?
CHARLES: I don't blush. Look, I have to go. It was great meeting you. I hope you have a great career as a hairdresser. If you're ever in Manhattan, look me up.
DENNIS: Thanks, I will. Maybe you can take me to my first opera.
CHARLES: It's a deal.

(Charles starts to leave.)

DENNIS: Here, you forgot your picture.
CHARLES: You keep it.
DENNIS: Well, then, here take this.

(Dennis goes to the box and pulls out a cup.)

(Continued) I have so many and maybe when you use it, you'll think of this San Diego afternoon.

CHARLES: No, it's yours. I'd hate to break up the set. Bring it with you if you visit.
DENNIS: By the time I get to Manhattan you'll have forgotten all about me.
CHARLES: No, I won't. I can't forget that face.
DENNIS: 70's charm?
CHARLES: Maybe.
DENNIS: How long before you would need a decision?
CHARLES: I think you've already made up your mind.
DENNIS: This is crazy. I can't do this.
CHARLES: Why not?
DENNIS: If there is one thing you should know about me is that I'm really not a spontaneous person.
CHARLES: Not spontaneous? I've known you for five hours and I've already seen you naked. *(They both laugh.)* There ya go, there's that cute smile. When I moved to Manhattan I was scared out of my mind, but it changed my life. It was the best decision I ever made. Let me show you how to live.
DENNIS: Okay.
CHARLES: Okay?
DENNIS: Just please don't make me regret this.

(Charles kisses Dennis, after a moment he pulls away.)

(Continued) But, if we are going to do this, we are doing it as friends.

CHARLES: Deal. *(Kisses Dennis on top of the head.)* Friends.

> *(Charles takes the cup that Dennis has been holding.)*

(Continued) Your plane leaves in a week.

(Music. He leaves. Dennis is left sitting on the bed.)

END OF SCENE

Act 1

Scene 2

(The set has a table with two wig styling stations for Dennis and Edward. There is a shelf with wigs. There is a small table with a phone. There are two makeup chairs. Dennis & Edward are styling wigs in the studio. They are smoking. Edward is styling a wig for an Opera and Dennis is styling a hairpiece for Charles' Mother Angela.)

EDWARD: ...right there outside the bar, I told him. I just can't keep doing this, if you want to be with me you have to leave your wife. I'm not just going to be your little secret anymore. I mean it's the 70's right? The gay revolution is here and it's real honey. Pull back the veil and come out.
DENNIS: Yeah, but aren't you still legally married Jenny?
EDWARD: Separated. That really doesn't matter, besides this isn't about me. This is about him and his inability to accept who he really is.
DENNIS: Maybe you should try meeting someone outside of a backroom.
EDWARD: That's not really the point. Bitch, what's wrong with you today?
DENNIS: I'm nervous. Charles isn't here yet and his mother is coming into town.
EDWARD: So.
DENNIS: So? What do you mean so? I'm nervous if I don't get her hairpiece right, I'm going to die of embarrassment.

EDWARD: Girl.
DENNIS: Girl what?
EDWARD: Stop being so dramatic. His mother is not that bad. I've met her, she's kind of amazing. She's like a mix between Joan Crawford and Bette Davis. Well, if they were born in upstate New York.
DENNIS: And that's supposed to make me feel better? You just described the two biggest divas in the entire history of Hollywood and that is supposed make me calm me down? *(Pause.)* You know how much she means to him.
EDWARD: Girl, you need a Quaalude. Relax. He'll be here soon.

(Scene shifts to Charles' apartment. We see the mug Dennis gave Charles in scene one on the shelf. Charles and a hustler named Brian enter his bedroom.)

BRIAN: Wow, this place is pretty groovy. I've never been in an apartment on Riverside Drive before. I don't spend a lot of time outside of 42nd street.
CHARLES: Or Central Park?
BRIAN: Maybe. Do you care if I smoke?
CHARLES: No. Let me get you an ashtray.

(Charles exits. The hustler takes off his jacket and sits on the bed. Charles comes back.)

BRIAN: You want one?
CHARLES: Thanks, but I don't smoke.
BRIAN: You don't?

CHARLES: I know it's hard to believe but not everyone smokes.

(Brian stands up and looks out the window.)

BRIAN: You have a pretty impressive view from your window.
CHARLES: That's why I wanted this apartment. The view of the sunrise is amazing.
BRIAN: I'd like to see it sometime.
CHARLES: I don't know about that, that's reserved for a select few.
BRIAN: Is that so? Well, maybe if we didn't meet in Central Park, I'd have the privilege of that view huh?
CHARLES: Maybe. Maybe, not.
BRIAN: You know you're kind of irritating.
CHARLES: You can leave if you want to.
BRIAN: Then you would win and then you would miss out.
CHARLES: Miss out? I don't have much time. You're going to have to impress me with all your tricks pretty quick.
BRIAN: Do you think you can keep up with me?
CHARLES: You have no idea kid.

(Charles goes to the phone and dials. The lights return on the studio. The phone rings.)

DENNIS: Elsen and Associates.
CHARLES: Hey it's me.
DENNIS: Where are you?
CHARLES: At my apartment.

25

DENNIS: What are you doing there? Your mother is going to be here any minute.

(During the phone conversation the hustler takes out a small vial of cocaine and a spoon, he does a bump. He strips down to his underwear for Charles and starts unbuttoning Charles shirt and pants.)

CHARLES: I got held up at the Met. I had to swing home for a minute.
DENNIS: Is everything alright? We didn't lose the contract did we?
CHARLES: No, nothing like that. I won't be long, a half an hour at the most.
DENNIS: What am I supposed to do with your mother?

(Brian offers Charles a bump of coke.)

CHARLES: No thanks.
DENNIS: No thanks what?
CHARLES: Huh, what?
DENNIS: Wait a minute. Are you with a guy?
CHARLES: Maybe.
DENNIS: You have got to be kidding me.
CHARLES: Relax.

(Angela enters unseen by Dennis. Edward sees her)

DENNIS: How am I supposed to relax!? I can't believe you are doing this today. Your trick better be worth it!
EDWARD: Angela, how are you?

ANGELA: I'm good Edward how are you?
EDWARD: Where's Roy?

(Dennis notices Angela. Into the phone.)

DENNIS: She's here.
ANGELA: He decided to stay home, his mother isn't feeling well.
EDWARD: I'm sorry to hear that.
DENNIS: You must be Angela, I'm Dennis.
ANGELA: Pleasure to meet you. Where's Charles?
DENNIS: He's running a little late.

(Dennis returns to the phone conversation.)

(Continued) Yes, thank you so much. So, when should we expect the delivery?
CHARLES: I won't be long, I promise. Just put her hairpiece on and I'll be there before you're done.
DENNIS: And if the wigs aren't here by then do we get a refund, or can I come there and ram my fist down your throat?

(Edward and Angela gives Dennis a puzzled look. Charles laughs.)

(Continued) Sorry, I must have lost my head. We look forward to your business.
ANGELA: So, you're the Dennis I've been hearing so much about. Charles says you are an amazing wig stylist.
DENNIS: Thank you but it's easy when you have Charles' designs to work from.

ANGELA: Of course, I said stylist not designer.

(Angela crosses away from Edward and Dennis to look at the new studio.)

(Continued) Edward, how is your lovely wife?
EDWARD: She's doing well thank you.

(The next two lines should be said under Edward and Charles' breath)

DENNIS: Closet case.
EDWARD: Bitch.
ANGELA: I like this studio. It's nicer than Charles last place.
EDWARD: It is. The other one was so small. But with all the new clients he needed a larger space.
ANGELA: Is there coffee here?
DENNIS: No, but I can run out and get you a cup if you would like.
EDWARD: I'll do it.
DENNIS: It's no trouble I'll do it.
ANGELA: No let Edward, he knows how I like my coffee. That way we can get to know each other.
DENNIS: Of course.
EDWARD: I'll be back

(Edward exits. There is a small awkward pause between Dennis and Angela.)

DENNIS: How was your train ride?
ANGELA: I didn't take a train. Charles hired a car.
DENNIS: I'm sorry he didn't tell me.

ANGELA: Roy usually drives but Charles didn't want me riding a dirty Amtrak train alone.
DENNIS: That was very nice of him.
ANGELA: Well, I am his mother.
DENNIS: Yes.

(Angela walks up to the wig table.)

ANGELA: Is this my hairpiece? Charles said you were setting one for me.
DENNIS: It is. I hope you like it.
ANGELA: It's a little big, but I guess we won't know until you put it on me, right?
DENNIS: Right.

(Dennis nervously turns to the table and starts to take the hairpiece off the wig block.)

(Continued) Well, if you want to wait for Charles we can, or I can put it on you now.
ANGELA: Now would be good.

(Angela sits.)

DENNIS: Ok, have a seat.

(Dennis turns and noticed that she has already sat down.)

(Continued) Okay.
ANGELA: Can you get me an ashtray please?
DENNIS: Sure.

(Dennis hands her the one he and Edward were using.)

ANGELA: A clean one.
DENNIS: Of course.

(Dennis exits. Angela calls to him offstage.)

ANGELA: Did Charles say how long he was going to be?

(Dennis enters. He hands her the ashtray. Dennis starts to attach Angela's hairpiece and style it on her head during the following dialogue.)

DENNIS: He said a half an hour at the most. His meeting ran late. We've been so busy lately with the Met and the all the traveling.
ANGELA: We? Are you traveling with Charles?
DENNIS: I meant the company, Charles' company. He's taking on so many clients that he has to send different teams out to operas all over the country.
ANGELA: So, you don't always go where he goes then?
DENNIS: No, I do. He takes me with him because he does the big operas, and they have the most wigs.
ANGELA: I see. Well, he keeps you pretty close then.
DENNIS: Yes *(Pause.)* Angela, I consider him a very close friend. He has done a lot for me. I would never have this amazing career without him.
ANGELA: I know that. I just like to make sure his company is being protected and he's not being

(Continued) taken advantage of. Charles has worked very hard to build this company to what it is today, and I would hate to see him lose that.

DENNIS: We all only have Charles best interest at heart.
ANGELA: That's good.

(Angela gets a quick glance of her hairpiece in the mirror.)

(Continued) It's still a too big.

(Dennis starts to fix it. He is feeling a little less nervous.)

DENNIS: Sorry. I bet you can't wait to see Charles' new apartment. It's beautiful.
ANGELA: Any apartment is better than his last one. I can't imagine how he and his roommate lived in such a small studio apartment.
DENNIS: It was tiny. That couch was so uncomfortable.
ANGELA: Excuse me?
DENNIS: When Charles moved me here from California I moved into John and Charles' apartment.
ANGELA: How exactly did that work?
DENNIS: What do you mean?
ANGELA: Charles told me they took turns sleeping on the couch.
DENNIS: He did?
ANGELA: Yes, he did.

DENNIS: Well, we all kind of took turns on the bed, couch, and the floor. It saved a lot of money.
ANGELA: I bet it did.
DENNIS: It wasn't for long. After a couple months I found my own place.
ANGELA: How is John? Charles doesn't talk about him much anymore.
DENNIS: He's good. He met someone and they are very happy.
ANGELA: Really? What's her name?
DENNIS: He didn't say.
ANGELA: Interesting.

(Dennis tries to change the subject.)

DENNIS: Well, anyway Charles' new place is beautiful. Riverside Drive is such a great neighborhood.
ANGELA: He told me. Maybe someday you'll be able to move to a neighborhood like that.
DENNIS: I already have. The apartment next to his was open so I said, "why not" and I moved in.

(Shocked look from Angela just as Edward walks in with the coffee and a shopping bag.)

EDWARD: Sorry it took so long.

(Edward takes a scarf out of the bag)

(Continued) I saw this amazing scarf in a store window, and I had to have it.

ANGELA: It's beautiful. Your wife is going to love it.

(Angela takes the coffee cup.)

(Continued) My coffee is cold.

(Angela hands it back to Edward)

(Continued) Be a dear and get me another one.

EDWARD: Um. Okay. I'll be right back.

(Edward sensing the tension exits.)

DENNIS: Did I say something wrong?
ANGELA: Next door?
DENNIS: That was Charles' idea.
ANGELA: Can I ask you a question? Do you think I'm stupid? Do you?
DENNIS: I'm sorry. I don't know what you are talking about.
ANGELA: Just friends huh? Dennis, I think it's very obvious that there's more to your friendship than you're letting on.
DENNIS: Charles is just my friend.
ANGELA: You really think that I believe that? Charles calls me one day and all he can talk about is this new guy named Dennis and then all of a sudden John is gone.
DENNIS: I had nothing to do with that. I didn't even think that you knew about Charles and John.
ANGELA: I'm his Mother. How would I not know?

DENNIS: Every time Charles is on the phone with his father, he tells him he too busy to have a girlfriend. I just assumed you both didn't know.
ANGELA: You shouldn't assume things. Charles never told me I just knew.
DENNIS: How did you know?
ANGELA: When he comes home to visit, he and his cousin Joanne go out bar hopping. Then the next morning there is a new "friend" at the table for breakfast. My husband may turn a blind eye but I'm not some hick from upstate New York.
DENNIS: I didn't think you were. *(Pause.)* I can assure you that we are just friends. I would never hurt Charles. I owe him everything. If, anything I'm very protective of him.
ANGELA: Good, keep it that way. I'm counting on you to keep an eye on him.

(Edward enters with the coffee.)

EDWARD: Here's your coffee.
ANGELA: Thank you Edward.

(Without even tasting the coffee Angela takes the coffee cup and drops it in the wastepaper basket.)

(Continued) Well boys, it looks like Charles isn't getting here anytime soon. I have an idea, let's go grab a drink and do some shopping.
DENNIS: But we have some wigs that still need to be set.

ANGELA: Charles won't care. I'll talk to him. *(As they are leaving.)* By the way Edward that scarf won't go with that outfit.

(Edward and Angela both laugh as they leave. Dennis follows behind shaking his head. Scene shifts to Charles Bedroom. Charles and the Hustler have just finished having sex.)

CHARLES: Well, that was interesting. Where did a young kid like you learn to do that? 42nd St?
BRIAN: Ohio.
CHARLES: You're from Ohio?
BRIAN: Are you surprised?
CHARLES: You don't look like a country boy.
BRIAN: Not everyone from Ohio looks like a farmer.
CHARLES: Well, next time I'm in Ohio I better start cruising the cornfields then.
BRIAN: I wouldn't do that unless you want to get your ass kicked. Besides not all of Ohio is covered in farms.
CHARLES: Pretty rough there for a gay kid huh?
BRIAN: It wasn't too bad as long as you didn't flaunt it which I never did. That made me pretty popular with the guys in our town park bathroom. Then my father found out and kicked me out of the house. He packed me a bag and gave me fifty bucks to leave town. I was on the next train to Manhattan.
CHARLES: Shit, it's five o'clock. Listen I have to go.
BRIAN: Do I get to see you again?

35

CHARLES: We'll see. Ya, know you're very attractive.
BRIAN: Thank you.
CHARLES: I have to get a picture of you.
BRIAN: A picture? For what?
CHARLES: I don't want to forget my little Ohio boy.
BRIAN: I have a name. Brian.
CHARLES: Well, Brian, strike a pose and smile.

(Brian holds up the bedsheet. Just as Charles snaps the Polaroid picture Dennis walks in.)

BRIAN: Hi.
DENNIS: Oh my God.
CHARLES: Oh, hey.
DENNIS: Oh, hey? Is that all you can say is oh, hey?
CHARLES: What's wrong?
DENNIS: What's wrong?! While you were here banging this trick, I was shopping at Macy's with your mother and Edward.
CHARLES: Really?

(Charles starts laughing.)

DENNIS: This isn't funny.
BRIAN: Actually, it kind of is.
DENNIS: Yeah, well, street trade no one asked you.
CHARLES: His name is Brian.
DENNIS: Are you serious right now?
BRIAN: I have to piss.

(Brian exits with the bedsheet wrapped around his waist. After he leaves Charles goes to the bed and gets a photo album from under the mattress. He opens it and finds a place to put Brian's picture in it.)

DENNIS: I can't believe you did this to me. You knew how nervous I was to meet your mother.
CHARLES: Can you relax please?
DENNIS: No, I can't. You know in the first five minutes of meeting her she accused me of breaking up you and John.
CHARLES: She did?

(Charles starts laughing again.)

DENNIS: Stop laughing. What are you doing?
CHARLES: Putting Brian's picture in my man book.
DENNIS: You have a photo album with pictures of your tricks?
CHARLES: Only the good ones.
DENNIS: Jesus Christ Charles

(Dennis starts looking at the picture album.)

(Continued) Oh my god, I'm surprised you can walk after that one.

CHARLES: Have you been drinking?
DENNIS: Yes.
CHARLES: You don't drink.

DENNIS: Well, I did today because after we went shopping your mother wanted a drink and Edward in all his stupidity suggested we go to Stud Bar.
CHARLES: You took my mother to The Stud?
DENNIS: No, Edward did. I said, "that's probably not the kind of bar you would like." She looked at me like I slapped her in the face and said, "I can go anywhere I would like, come on Edward let's go to The Stud!" We sat at the bar, Edward disappeared into the backroom, and I was left sitting at the bar with your mother. After her fourth martini she decided Edward must not be coming back and that she wanted me to "take her to Charles apartment."
CHARLES: Where is she now?
DENNIS: In your living room.
CHARLES: Are you kidding me? Brian just walked in there wearing a bedsheet!
DENNIS: You should have thought about that before you picked up a trick in Central Park!

(Angela Enters.)

ANGELA: Hello Charles.

(Charles kisses her on the cheek.)

CHARLES: Hello Mother.
ANGELA: You look good. I'm starving. I want to go out to eat.
CHARLES: Ok. I just have to say goodbye to my friend.
ANGELA: Brian? That kid from Ohio?
CHARLES: Yes.

ANGELA: I invited him.
DENNIS: Oh dear God.
ANGELA: Dennis, did you say something?
DENNIS: No, I was just clearing my throat.
ANGELA: Ok good. Now Charles, I want Italian, good Italian. Does Brian like Italian?
DENNIS: Apparently.
ANGELA: Excuse me Dennis?
CHARLES: He does. Mother why don't you go and wait in the living room, we'll leave in a few minutes.
ANGELA: Hurry up Charles, I don't want to wait too long.
CHARLES: Ok.

(Angela starts to exit as Brian enters. They come face to face.)

ANGELA: And you, pants are not optional.
BRIAN: Got it.

(Brian and Charles start to get dressed.)

DENNIS: This is the Twilight Zone. Are we really going to dinner with your mother and some hustler?
BRIAN: I'm in the room.
DENNIS: I realize that.
CHARLES: Listen, it will be fine it's just dinner and then we will bring her to her hotel. Ok?
DENNIS: This is crazy.
CHARLES: But it's fun. Loosen up a little.
BRIAN: Yeah, loosen up.
DENNIS: No one's talking to you.

CHARLES: Stop it. Come on.

(Dennis and Charles start to leave.)

DENNIS: By the way your mother knows you're gay.
CHARLES: I know, my dykey cousin Joanne told her but that's alright because I told her parents about her and her gym teacher Mrs. Spinelli.

(Charles Exits. Dennis yells to Brian.)

DENNIS: Move your feet street trade!

(Music. Brian & Dennis exit.)

END OF SCENE

Act 1

Scene 3

(Charles is finishing up make-up on male baritone named Richard. Dennis & Edward are working on wigs. Charles is telling a story about one of his past flings. He is smoking.)

CHARLES: It was really great. There had to be six guys going at it at.
RICHARD: Six guys? Were you at the Continental Baths?
CHARLES: No, we were in Sydney Australia doing an opera and I snuck away for a bit. One of the stagehands told me about this bath house. It was huge; I swear there were about one hundred guys there. There was any type of guys you wanted. Young, old…
DENNIS: He left us with the hillbilly.
EDWARD: The Elsenettes had to entertain the little street trade while Charles was "finalizing" the contracts with the Sydney Opera.
RICHARD: The Elsenettes?
CHARLES: Yes, they think it's funny to call themselves the Elsenettes.
EDWARD: It's like he's Diana Ross and we're the Supremes.

(Dennis and Edward strike a Supremes like pose.)

CHARLES: Can we get back to the good story please?

DENNIS: Yes, please tell us all about the sweaty fun you had going down, down under.

CHARLES: Anyway, so they were all going at it, and I don't know what came over me, but I just jumped right it the middle. It was so hot. There were even leather guys.

EDWARD: Leather never really did it for me. All that elbow deep stuff scares the shit out of me and the thought of wearing a jock strap gives me horrible flashbacks of gym class.

RICHARD: I don't know jock straps are kind of hot.

CHARLES: Good to know. Anyway, it was really great.

DENNIS: Until he got home and had to face hurricane Brian.

CHARLES: I don't think that's really important.

(Carol, a Soprano enters. She is visibly upset.)

CAROL: Charles!

CHARLES: What's wrong?

CAROL: That director. I hate him! He has no artistic vision. It's just, go to the left and sing. Enter and sing. Sing and exit. I can't stand it anymore.

DENNIS: Carol you're doing amazing in the show.

CAROL: Thank you Dennis, but that jerk won't let bring anything new to this role. I want to do it in the nude like it's supposed to be done but he wants me to wear a stupid body stocking.

RICHARD: Carol, you know nothing you say is going to change his mind about the nude scene.

CAROL: What do you care? You could walk onstage, take a shit, and that bastard of a director would cum in his pants.

(They all look shocked. Charles laughs.)

RICHARD: Carol!
CAROL: Oh my God, I can't believe I said that. I'm sorry Richard.
DENNIS: Have you tried talking to him?
CAROL: No. I'm trying not to be difficult; I'm new to the business. I need the work.
EDWARD: Listen honey, it's not about being difficult.
CHARLES: I have an idea. I think it's time you spoke up for yourself. I think I know the perfect way to do that.
CAROL: What do you mean?
CHARLES: Sit down. Look, when I was at Julliard I watched the opera greats fight for what they wanted. Carol you deserve to be heard.
CAROL: I've already tried that Charles, he won't listen.
CHARLES: Then it's time to get creative. Let's stage a good old-fashioned diva fit.
DENNIS: Charles you're going to get her fired.
CHARLES: No, I'm not Dennis. Do you think Pavarotti and Beverly Sills got where they are today by settling for second best? *(To Carol.)* Do you trust me?
CAROL: I don't know. Richard, what do you think?
RICHARD: It couldn't hurt to try.
CAROL: Ok, I'm listening.

CHARLES: I'm going to go out there and tell everyone that you refuse to go on tonight unless you get to do the nude scene. Then you can come out, start yelling about the scene and your artistic views. Trust me it will work.
CAROL: I don't know if I can do that Charles. No one would believe it.
CHARLES: That's the whole point. Come on Richard can help.
RICHARD: You can do this Carol. Just play the part.
CAROL: Ok.
CHARLES: Let's go.

(Richard, Carol, and Charles exit.)

DENNIS: That's a little crazy.
EDWARD: If she gets her way it will be worth it. Besides you love it when Charles stirs the pot, then you get to walk into the room and calm things down.
DENNIS: What does that mean?
EDWARD: Nothing, I'm just saying that maybe you like drama as much as Charles likes to bang street trade.
DENNIS: Bitch don't get crazy. I don't like it that much.
EDWARD: Does Charles seem a little out of control lately?
DENNIS: I don't know. We've been on the road so much I think we've all been acting a little crazy.
EDWARD: But he's smoking now.

DENNIS: We have no room to talk we both smoke. We can't judge him for that.

(Brian enters unseen by Dennis and Edward.)

EDWARD: He's so different since the hillbilly has been around.
BRIAN: The hillbilly has a name.
EDWARD: Well Dennis I'm going to the bathroom I all of a sudden have the urge to take a shit.

(Edward exits.)

BRIAN: Wow, he really doesn't like me does he?
DENNIS: It doesn't matter, Charles likes you.
BRIAN: Do you like me?
DENNIS: Like I said Charles likes you.
BRIAN: I don't understand you and Edward. I've never done anything to you, and you treat me like shit.
DENNIS: Listen, Charles is my best friend, and we look out for each other. I have my guard up when it comes to his men, and you are the first trick that actually has stuck around.
BRIAN: Would you please stop calling me a trick! I'm so sick of that. Trick, street trade, hooker, hustler. It's so funny how you forgot it was Charles who picked me up.
DENNIS: Yeah, in Central Park.
BRIAN: Jesus Christ have you ever been to the Rambles?
DENNIS: No, I haven't.

BRIAN: Maybe you should go there sometime and see for yourself just what it's like.
DENNIS: It's not really my scene.
BRIAN: Well for your information I didn't plan on going home with anyone that day. I was just passing through. I saw Charles with another guy, and we locked eyes and he pushed the guy away. I walked away and he followed me. It just sort of happened.
DENNIS: Why are you telling me this?
BRIAN: Because I want you to treat me like a human and not just a piece of fucking trash.

(Charles and Richard run in.)

DENNIS: What are you doing?
CHARLES: Shhh.

(Carol enters, she is yelling.)

CAROL: I guess you all didn't know who you were dealing with. I'm not as sweet as I look and if you think for one minute I'm not doing that scene in the nude you must be crazy!

(Carol turns to everyone and they all break down laughing.)

RICHARD: Oh my God Carol you were fabulous. Dennis, you missed it. Carol was fabulous. It was the most amazing thing I've ever seen.
DENNIS: Congratulations, I guess.

CHARLES: Now we just need to get this story out to the press. They would eat up a story like this. I know what we can do. That strip club down the street…

(Richard interrupts.)

RICHARD: The Pink Purse or the Sticky Nipple?
CHARLES: The Pink Purse, they've gotten picketed at least three times since we've been in town. I'll send Edward down there to tell them you are going onstage nude tonight and see if we can get the strippers to picket opening night.
CAROL: Do you think they would do that?
CHARLES: Who knows but it couldn't hurt to try.
CAROL: I can't believe this. This is so crazy.
RICHARD: Carol let's go into the balcony and see if the director is still freaking out.

(Carol and Richard exit.)

CHARLES: Brian, give me a bump.
DENNIS: A bump?
BRIAN: Coke.
DENNIS: I realize that Brian. I just didn't realize that Charles was into that stuff.
CHARLES: Every once in a while. Do you want some?
DENNIS: I'm going to head to stage left and set the quick-change wigs.
CHARLES: Don't worry about it, with all this excitement they are not starting on time tonight.

DENNIS: If they do I want to be ready.
CHARLES: Are you okay?
DENNIS: I'm fine.
CHARLES: No, you're not.

(Dennis shoots a look at Brian.)

DENNIS: I don't want to talk about this right now.
BRIAN: Don't mind me.
CHARLES: Can you give us a minute?
BRIAN: Sure.

(Brian walks over to the wig styling station and does a line. Brian leaves the vial on the table.)

(Continued) I'll just leave this here.

(Brian leaves.)

CHARLES: What's going on with you?
DENNIS: Me? What's going on with you?
CHARLES: What are you talking about? The coke?
DENNIS: It's not just the coke. It's the coke, it's the hustler, the cigarettes...
CHARLES: You smoke!
DENNIS: Yes, but it's not like you.
CHARLES: I don't know what your problem with Brian is.
DENNIS: He's a trick you picked up!
CHARLES: So, what! People meet in all different ways.

DENNIS: That's fine but this kid is head over heels for you. When you go off to fuck someone Edward and I are stuck lying for you.
CHARLES: What do you want me to do? You know I've always been like that and I'm not changing for anyone.
DENNIS: Charles, no one wants you to change who you are, but you have to be honest with him. I don't care if you want to have your cake and eat it too but just be honest with him.
CHARLES: I will.
DENNIS: Fine!
CHARLES: Fine!

(Charles is smiling at Dennis.)

DENNIS: What are you smiling at?
CHARLES: You're acting like my mother.
DENNIS: Are you serious with that? You're such a bitch!
CHARLES: What?
DENNIS: What? You just compared me to your mother!
CHARLES: I'm sorry.
DENNIS: You are so going to pay for that one. The next time you are off banging some piece of street trade I'm bringing Ohio Boy there.

(Dennis starts to exit and Charles is following.)

CHARLES: Now who's being a bitch?
DENNIS: I'd be careful what you say right now.

(Music.)

END OF SCENE

Act 1

Scene 4

(Charles is working on Richard's makeup again and Dennis is fixing Richard's hair)

DENNIS: Have you called James back at the Cincinnati Opera about La Traviata? He called three times last week.
CHARLES: I'll call him tomorrow.
DENNIS: And what about this "On Your Toes" revival?
CHARLES: What about it?
DENNIS: I thought you said you didn't want to do musicals.
CHARLES: It could be big for us. Musicals are getting popular again and this would open doors for us.
DENNIS: But "On Your Toes" is kind of old fashioned, isn't it?
CHARLES: It doesn't matter, it's a start trust me.
DENNIS: You're the boss. Where's Edward?
CHARLES: I sent him to the apartment to get our tuxedos for the party.
DENNIS: I thought Brian was doing that.

(No response from Charles.)

(Continued) What? Another fight?
CHARLES: I don't want to talk about this right now.
RICHARD: Don't mind me.

CHARLES: It's not you Richard. I just have a lot of things on my mind today with opening night and my mother in town. We have twelve operas in the next four months, and I just feel a little overwhelmed.
DENNIS: And I'm sure Brian isn't helping.
CHARLES: Dennis, please.
DENNIS: Fine.

(Edward enters.)

EDWARD: Sorry it took me so long I ran into Brian. By the way you're welcome Charles, I calmed him down. You two aren't getting a divorce anytime soon.
CHARLES: What did you say?
EDWARD: I told him you were working late at the studio with us last night and that's why you didn't come home until 5am. I don't understand why it matters anyway you never cared what your hustlers thought before.
DENNIS: It's been two years. I think he's past the hustler stage by now.

(We hear the overture to "La Boheme.")

RICHARD: That's my cue. *(Under his breath.)* Thank God.

(Richard exits.)

DENNIS: Have a great show Richard.

EDWARD: I put the tuxedos in the other room. I have to go get ready for the quick changes. Do you want me to meet your mother after curtain call and bring her to the party?
CHARLES: Yes, and we'll meet you there once we are all set here.

(Edward starts to exit.)

(Continued) Bring her right to the party. No pit stops.
EDWARD: Okay.

(Edward exits.)

DENNIS: Are you sure you're alright?
CHARLES: I'm fine I'm just tired.
DENNIS: Well, you shouldn't have stayed up so late last night, slut.
CHARLES: You should talk.
DENNIS: Me? I was in bed in early.
CHARLES: Were you?
DENNIS: Yes, I was.
CHARLES: I saw you.
DENNIS: You saw me where?
CHARLES: In the park. The rambles. It's ok.

(Charles lights a cigarette and sits in the makeup chair.)

DENNIS: I've never done that before. It's just after we left the studio last night and you said you were grabbing a night cap I knew where you were going.

(Continued) I just followed you. I almost turned around a couple times, but you always talked about the rambles like it was the best place on earth. When I was following you, I looked up and the sky was so clear, it was the perfect night. When you walked into the park, I waited a couple minutes and then I went in.
CHARLES: And?
DENNIS: It was amazing. You know me I'm not like that, but I just felt so free.
CHARLES: Was it just one?
DENNIS: Yes. He was very nice, I told him it was my first time in the park. He was very sweet. It was kind of romantic. I'm guessing it's not usually like that.
CHARLES: Oh God no, it's never like that. It's a place to find a quick little treat and be done with it. They never stick around. You occasionally see them there again or you randomly see them walking in Manhattan with their wives.

(Dennis starts to cry.)

(Continued) Why are you crying?
DENNIS: I don't know.
CHARLES: Just breath and relax.
DENNIS: The person that followed you into the park last night is not me. That's not what I want.
CHARLES: I know that, but it's ok to let yourself be free every once in a while.
DENNIS: I can't be that person. I want to be with someone.

CHARLES: Then date someone. I worry about you. You never date anyone and when you, Edward and I go to the bars you always go home alone.
DENNIS: Charles, I'm not like you. You walk into The Stud, order a drink and within ten minutes you have the cutest guy in the bar wrapped around your little finger. I can't do that.
CHARLES: You don't have to do that. I've been with hundreds of men. I'm dating someone I met in Central Park, but I sleep with at least three other guys every week. Do you really want that? There's going to be a time in my life when that it is going to get old.

(Brian enters unseen by Charles and Dennis.)

(Continued) Don't look up to me when it comes to men, I may look happy but I'm not.

(Charles touches Dennis' face.)

BRIAN: Well, this is great.
CHARLES: Brian…
BRIAN: You son-of-a-bitch. You're not happy?
CHARLES: That's not what I meant.
BRIAN: But it's what you said.
DENNIS: Maybe I should leave.
BRIAN: No. Stay. You looked pretty comfortable there a second ago.
DENNIS: What are you talking about?
BRIAN: You know exactly what I'm talking about Dennis.

(Angela enters.)

ANGELA: Charles?
CHARLES: Mother what are you doing back here?
ANGELA: You know I hate the La Boheme. I got bored. Hello Dennis, Brian.
DENNIS: Angela.
BRIAN: Your son is an Asshole.
CHARLES: Jesus Brian!
ANGELA: How dare you speak to me like that! What's going on here?
BRIAN: Ask your son and his boyfriend.

(Brian flips off Dennis and exits.)

ANGELA: Charles what is he talking about?
CHARLES: Nothing. I'll be right back.

(Charles exits.)

ANGELA: Isn't anyone going to tell me what's going on?
DENNIS: Brian has the wrong idea about something.
ANGELA: I see.
DENNIS: It's nothing.
ANGELA: You look like you've been crying.
DENNIS: I've had a very long day. I'm tired.
ANGELA: Do you have an ashtray?

(Dennis grabs the dirty ashtray from the table and brings it to her.)

DENNIS: Yes, but it's not a clean one. We also have coffee but it's cold, I don't have time to run and get you a hot cup either.
ANGELA: You seem on edge.

(Dennis puts the ashtray down.)

(Continued) After all these years, do I still make you nervous?
DENNIS: A little.
ANGELA: Come on Dennis, you've spent the past couple Christmas' with our family, and I still make you nervous? I'm not a bad person.
DENNIS: I know.
ANGELA: Then relax a little. Any ashtray is fine.

(Charles enters with Edward. Charles has a bloody lip. He was just in a fistfight with Brian. Charles is yelling.)

CHARLES: That mother fucker! I'll break his neck!
ANGELA: What happened?
DENNIS: Oh my god.
CHARLES: It's nothing.
ANGELA: Nothing? You're bleeding.
EDWARD: The stage manager came and got me. Charles and Brian were beating each other up outside the stage door. You're lucky no one else saw you, we could lose this contract.
ANGELA: Edward, please
DENNIS: Get me a towel.

(Dennis sits Charles down and tends to his wounds.)

CHARLES: It's fine, it's just a little cut.
ANGELA: It's not fine. It's gushing.
DENNIS: You might need a stitch.
EDWARD: I told you I never trusted that little piece of shit.
CHARLES: Stop it! All of you. *(Silence.)* Edward, get backstage.

(Edward storms off.)

(Continued) Mother, can you please just go back to your seat. Edward will bring you to the party after the show and we'll meet you there.
ANGELA: I'm not going to the party. I didn't come all the way here to be yelled at. I'll be at my hotel.

(Angela exits.)

CHARLES: Dennis, don't you have some wigs that need to be fixed before act two?!
DENNIS: Yes.
CHARLES: My lip is fine. *(Pause.)* I'm sorry I yelled at you.
DENNIS: It's ok. Although I don't think your mother is going to forgive you that easily. Let her go to the hotel, when I'm done with the wigs I'll go and talk to her.

(We hear "*Musetta's Waltz." We see Carol dressed a Musetta from La Boheme. She sings the first verse of Musetta's Waltz.)

(Continued) Here, take the towel. I'm going to go wash my hands.

(Dennis starts to leave.)

CHARLES: You still think my love life is fun?
DENNIS: I never thought it was.

(Dennis leaves. Charles is left sitting by himself. He takes out a vial and does some coke as the lights go down.)

*If the actress playing Carol is not a singer playing a musical track of Musetta's Waltz is just as effective.

END OF ACT ONE

Act 2

Scene 1

(Dennis and Edward are doing their usual routine of styling wigs.)

EDWARD: …apparently down to his knee but I told Charles, I said I don't care how hung he is he's not worth it.
DENNIS: And you really think he'll listen to either one of us about men?
EDWARD: No but at least he'll hear me. Besides he hasn't really dated anyone since Brian.
DENNIS: When has Charles ever really dated anyone? He should just install a turnstile. *(They laugh.)* Maybe someday he'll settle down.
EDWARD: Speaking of settling down.
DENNIS: Yes?
EDWARD: David?
DENNIS: Eh.
EDWARD: Kind of fizzled out, huh?
DENNIS: He's a great guy just not for me.

(Charles enters. He has takeout tray of coffee and a newspaper.)

CHARLES: Hey girls. How goes it?
EDWARD: Well thanks to us the wigs are almost set for La Traviata and we are just about to start with the wigs for "On Your Toes."
CHARLES: Did the director send over the notes?

DENNIS: Yes, he wants a lot of changes, but it should be fine.
CHARLES: Ok.
DENNIS: Where were you? Did you get lost in the park?
CHARLES: No, I had a meeting.
DENNIS: With whom?
CHARLES: An old friend.
DENNIS: An old friend?
CHARLES: Yes.
DENNIS: Anyone we know?
CHARLES: Maybe.
DENNIS: Interesting, Edward are you buying this line of bullshit coming out of his mouth?
EDWARD: Not at all.
CHARLES: Alright, I had breakfast with Brian.
DENNIS: Are you are kidding me? After everything he put you through you had breakfast with him. You almost lost your contract with the Met over that fist fight.
CHARLES: He's changed. He doesn't drink anymore and he's going to school now.
DENNIS: Well, isn't that nice.
CHARLES: I think the year apart helped us.
DENNIS: Us? Edward, are you hearing this?
EDWARD: Yes, and I have no comment. I didn't like him then and I don't think any amount of time can change that.
CHARLES: Well, you better start soon because he's stopping by in a couple minutes.
DENNIS: Why?
CHARLES: I wanted you to see how he's changed.

DENNIS: Were you even going to say anything or were you just going to let him show up and say, "oh hey!"
CHARLES: Why can't you two trust me? He's changed for the better.
EDWARD: I don't know Charles. This is coming out of nowhere.
DENNIS: Are you getting back with him?
CHARLES: I think so.
DENNIS: And nothing we can say will stop you?
CHARLES: Probably not.
DENNIS: So, we'll just have to accept it then?
CHARLES: It looks that way.
DENNIS: Fine.
EDWARD: Fine? Dennis you can't be serious.
DENNIS: Edward we aren't the ones dating him and if he's really different then it will be fine. *(To Charles.)* But don't think for one minute that we are going to cover for you anymore. If you want to go play in the Rambles or a bathhouse and Brian asks us where you are, you are on your own.
CHARLES: Thank you Dennis.
EDWARD: This is nuts. If you'll excuse me, I'll just be over here with my coffee and my newspaper while you two are off in la la land.
DENNIS: Ignore her. She just jealous because she hasn't got laid in three months.
EDWARD: I'm still in the room bitch.
DENNIS: Just keep your nose in your newspaper. When's he going to be here?
CHARLES: Soon. I told him I would come and talk to you first.
DENNIS: Clearly you don't need my approval.

CHARLES: I know. I swear he's...
DENNIS: Changed? Yeah I heard you the first twenty times.
EDWARD: Hey, you need to listen to this.
DENNIS: What? Did Archie and Veronica break up?
EDWARD: Can you be serious for a minute and listen?
DENNIS: I doubt it.
EDWARD: Rare Cancer Seen in 41 Homosexuals. Doctors in New York and California have diagnosed among homosexual men 41 cases of a rare and often rapidly fatal form of cancer. Eight of the victims died less than 24 months after the diagnosis was made. The cause of the outbreak is unknown, and there is as yet no evidence of contagion. But the doctors who have made the diagnoses, mostly in New York City and the San Francisco Bay area, are alerting other physicians who treat large numbers of homosexual men to the problem in an effort to help identify more cases.
DENNIS: Jesus.
EDWARD: The sudden appearance of the cancer, called Kaposi's sarcoma, usually appears first in spots on the legs and the disease took a slow course of up to 10 years. But these recent cases have shown that it appears in one or more violet-colored spots anywhere on the body. The spots can often be mistaken for bruises, sometimes appear as lumps and can turn brown after a period of time. The cancer often causes swollen lymph glands, and then kills by spreading throughout the body. Doctors at nine medical centers in New York and seven

(Continued) hospitals in California have been diagnosing the condition among younger men, all of whom said in the course of interviews that they were homosexual. Nine of the 41 cases known in California, and several of those victims reported that they had been in New York in the period preceding the diagnosis. The reporting doctors said that most cases had involved homosexual men who have had multiple and frequent sexual encounters with different partners, as many as 10 sexual encounters each night up to four times a week. There is no apparent danger to non-homosexuals from contagion. No cases have been reported to date outside the homosexual community or in women."

CHARLES: Great, another reason to blame us.

EDWARD: Dr. Friedman-Kien said he had tested nine of the victims and found severe defects in their immunological systems. The patients had serious malfunctions of two types of cells called T and B cell lymphocytes, which have important roles in fighting infections and cancer.

CHARLES: Thanks for ruining the day Edward.

DENNIS: This doesn't scare you at all?

CHARLES: Come on, this is ridiculous. It's just a bunch of people trying to scare the "gays."

EDWARD: Charles, I think it's a little more serious than that. This is the New York Times not some Christian News Paper.

CHARLES: What page was it on?

EDWARD: Page twenty-one.

CHARLES: Do you really think you should worry about an article they put on page twenty-one?

DENNIS: They buried it on page twenty-one because the word Homosexual is in the title, and you know that. If the title said something about killing old ladies and children, it would be on the front cover.

(Brian enters.)

BRIAN: Hey everyone.
CHARLES: Hey.

(Charles Brian a hug and kiss.)

BRIAN: Hi Dennis.
DENNIS: Hi.
BRIAN: Did I come at a bad time?
CHARLES: No, Edward and Dennis are getting all upset over some stupid newspaper article.
BRIAN: Are you talking about the Times article?
DENNIS: Yes.
BRIAN: Everyone's talking about it in the village
DENNIS: You've read it?
BRIAN: Yes, this article has a bunch of people scared.
EDWARD: I have to get out of here.

(Edward exits. Charles call after him.)

CHARLES: Its fine, you don't have to get so crazy over this. I don't know what his problem is.
DENNIS: He's scared. I'm a little scared too.
CHARLES: Stop it. This is nothing.
BRIAN: I don't know Charles.

CHARLES: I don't want to talk about this anymore. I'm not going to let some stupid newspaper article dictate how I live my life, and neither should you. I'm getting out of here. You two can sit here and wallow in your own misery.

(Charles storms off.)

BRIAN: Should I go talk to him?
DENNIS: No, I'd let him go cool off.

(There is small awkward pause between Dennis and Brian.)

BRIAN: So…
DENNIS: Yes?
BRIAN: I bet you thought you'd never see me again huh?
DENNIS: I always had a feeling you'd be back.
BRIAN: Really?
DENNIS: Yeah, they don't have a cure for herpes yet.
BRIAN: I guess some things never change.

(Brian starts to leave.)

DENNIS: Wait. Stop. I'm sorry.
BRIAN: Listen Dennis, we don't have to be friends. The only reason I came here is because Charles wanted me to. He wanted me to prove to you how much I…
DENNIS: Changed?
BRIAN: Yes.

DENNIS: I know, Charles told me a hundred times before you got here.
BRIAN: I told him that I didn't have to prove anything to you or Edward. I've never given you two any reason to hate me but you both made my life hell. You never gave me a chance.
DENNIS: What was I supposed to do Brian? He picked you up in Central Park.
BRIAN: Will you let that go! Who gives a fuck where we met? I was happy with him. I know I was a little crazy back then, but we all were.
DENNIS: I wasn't.
BRIAN: Well, excuse me. I'm not proud that I drank as much as did, but I've seen you drunk before.
DENNIS: But I never got out of control like you did. I would never jeopardize Charles career by starting a fight with him outside the Met of all places. That could have ruined him.
BRIAN: That wasn't my fault. *(Pause.)* Did he say I hit him first?
DENNIS: No.
BRIAN: But you just assumed it had to be me.

(Dennis is silent.)

DENNIS: I'm sorry.
BRIAN: It's ok. You're his best friend, it's what you're supposed to do. Let's just call it even.
DENNIS: Even for what?
BRIAN: I'm not going to lie, I was always jealous of your relationship with Charles. He never trusted me or opened up to me like he did to you.

DENNIS: Our relationships are very different. I'm the best friend, it's my job not to like you.
BRIAN: No, Charles' Mother's job is not to like me.
DENNIS: Her job is to not like anyone.
BRIAN: Do you think you can deal with me and Charles? Maybe try to be nice. Can you at least try that?
DENNIS: I can't guarantee anything.
BRIAN: Can I get a hug?
DENNIS: Don't push it street trade.

(Brian gives him a look.)

(Continued) Fine.

(Dennis hugs Brian. As he hugs him, he says.)

(Continued) If you hurt Charles, I will sell you to the highest bidding leather daddy I can find, you hear me?
BRIAN: Don't threaten me with a good time.

(Edward enters with a bottle of alcohol and sees them hugging.)

EDWARD: I don't even want to know.
DENNIS: It's alright Edward we like Brian now.
EDWARD: You like Brian, I don't.
DENNIS: Are you alright?
EDWARD: No, I'm not. I'm scared.
BRIAN: It's going to be ok, the doctors we'll figure this out.

EDWARD: Is this hooker really talking to me right now?
DENNIS: Edward calm down.
BRIAN: It's fine. I'm going to go find Charles.

(Brian exits. Edward calls after him.)

EDWARD: Try Central Park, you know your way around there!

(Edward starts chugging the alcohol.)

DENNIS: Stop it.
EDWARD: I can't believe you are doing this.
DENNIS: You're getting yourself all worked up.
EDWARD: That article describes me Dennis. *(He grabs the newspaper and reads.)* Frequent sexual encounters with different partners, as many as 10 sexual encounters each night up to four times a week. *(Crying but still trying to be funny.)* That's me. I'm a slut.
DENNIS: That's not you. That's not even Charles and he's a slut.
EDWARD: That isn't funny. *(Starts laughing.)* Ok, maybe it's a little funny.

(Music. His laughing turns to tears. Dennis hugs him.)

END OF SCENE

Act 2

Scene 2

(Charles enters in his bathrobe with a towel. Dennis is in the studio with Edward working on wigs. Dennis is styling a wig for Angela. The Studio is in half light. Charles pulls on his boxer shorts and takes of his bath robe. Charles sits on the bed and looks at a visible lesion on the bottom of his foot. Brian enters.)

BRIAN: Where do you want to go for dinner?

(Brian sees the lesion on his foot.)

(Continued) What is that?
CHARLES: What's what?
BRIAN: On the bottom of your foot. Is that what I think that is? *(No response from Charles.)* Oh my god, it is isn't it?
CHARLES: Stop being paranoid, it's just a bruise.
BRIAN: No, it's not. It's a lesion. You have it don't you?
CHARLES: What are you talking about?
BRIAN: You know damn well what I'm talking about.

(Scene shifts to the studio.)

DENNIS: She should be here soon. I don't know why she likes to come to the studio and not Charles apartment.

EDWARD: Maybe she likes to see you first.
DENNIS: That's very funny. I think she's worried about running into one his "friends". Maybe I should tell her there haven't been a lot of new "friends" lately.
EDWARD: Yeah, he's kind of slowed down huh? Well, we've all slowed down. What show is that wig for?
DENNIS: It's not for a show it's for his mother. She stopped wearing hair pieces and decided to go for full wigs.
EDWARD: Well, I guess if your son owns a wig company right? *(Small pause.)* Do you think Charles looks ok?
DENNIS: He looks fine. That cold he had just took it out of him.
EDWARD: That doesn't worry you at all?
DENNIS: Everything worries me now. He went to the doctors and got checked out. He's fine.

(Angela enters.)

ANGELA: Hello everyone.
EDWARD: Angela, how are you?
ANGELA: I'm doing good, thank you Edward.
DENNIS: Angela.
ANGELA: Dennis. You look well.
DENNIS: Thank you.

(Angela walks up to the wig table.)

ANGELA: So, is this my wig?
DENNIS: It is.

ANGELA: It's a little big don't you think? But then again you always make them too big.
DENNIS: But then I fix them before you leave and they're perfect.
ANGELA: Where's Charles?

(Scene shifts to Charles' apartment.)

BRIAN: You had that cold for three months. I thought you went to the doctor to get checked out.
CHARLES: I lied alright. I was sick of you and Dennis bugging me about it.
BRIAN: You haven't said anything to Dennis yet?
CHARLES: No. There is nothing to tell. I'm fine.
BRIAN: No, you're not. You're sick. This disease is real Charles, people are dying every day.
CHARLES: Shut up! Stop saying that.

(Charles goes into a coughing fit. He sits on the bed.)

BRIAN: I'm calling Dennis.
CHARLES: Please don't. My Mother is in town. I have to go to the studio.
BRIAN: No. Just sit there.

(Brian dials the phone. The phone rings in the studio. Dennis picks up the phone.)

DENNIS: Elsen and Associates.
BRIAN: Dennis, its Brian.
ANGELA: Is that Charles?

73

BRIAN: Is that Charles' mother? Don't let her know it's me.
DENNIS: No, Angela it's the Met. *(Into the phone.)* Is something wrong?
BRIAN: Yes. Can you come to Charles' apartment right now?
DENNIS: Of course, I'll be right over. *(He hangs up the phone.)* Angela, I'm sorry I have to run over to the Met. There's an emergency with a lace front on one of the wigs and they don't have time to bring it to the studio.
EDWARD: Why can't someone fix it there?
DENNIS: Because it's something I have to do. Can you fix Angela's wig for me? *(To Angela)* Once I'm done there I'll swing by Charles apartment and we'll meet you here, then we'll go to dinner.
ANGELA: Did Charles make reservations?
DENNIS: As far as I know he did.

(Dennis exits. The scene shifts back to the apartment)

BRIAN: What's taking him so long?
CHARLES: The studio isn't next door.
BRIAN: I can't believe you lied to me.
CHARLES: Can you please calm down?
BRIAN: I can't, not about this. You can't let something like this go. We've lost so many friends to this.
CHARLES: You're making a big deal about nothing. Can you just sit down please?

(Brian sits on the bed next to Charles.)

BRIAN: How can you be so calm?
CHARLES: What am I supposed to do? This could be nothing.

(We hear Dennis calling from offstage.)

DENNIS: Charles? Brian?
BRIAN: We're in here.

(Dennis enters.)

DENNIS: Sorry it took me so long. What's wrong?
CHARLES: Nothing, he's just acting crazy.
BRIAN: Show him.
DENNIS: Show me what?
CHARLES: Nothing.
BRIAN: I said show him God Dammit!

(Charles lifts up his foot and shows Dennis the lesion. There is silence.)

DENNIS: Oh my god Charles.
CHARLES: Don't look at me like that.
DENNIS: I thought you went to the doctors.
BRIAN: He lied.
DENNIS: Charles!
CHARLES: Don't. Don't do that. I'm not sick!
DENNIS: Okay…okay.
BRIAN: I still think you need to see a doctor. Can you at least do that please?
CHARLES: Fine, if it will make you two happy but there is nothing wrong.

(We hear Angela offstage.)

ANGELA: Charles?
CHARLES: What is she doing here?
DENNIS: I have no idea. I told her I would meet her back at the studio. She thinks I'm at the Met.
CHARLES: The Met?
DENNIS: Yes, I had to think quickly.
BRIAN: Finish getting dressed, I'll go out there and talk to her.
CHARLES: No. Don't. She doesn't know we're back together.
BRIAN: Jesus Christ Charles!
CHARLES: Give me a break she's not that easy to talk to.

(Angela enters, holding her wig.)

ANGELA: Charles? Oh, am I interrupting something?
CHARLES: Mother, no we were just about to leave to come back to the studio. What are you doing here?
ANGELA: I waited long enough besides Edward was doing a horrible job with my wig. That was a quick trip to the Met Dennis.
DENNIS: It was a quick fix.
ANGELA: I see. *(To Charles.)* Did you make reservations for dinner?
CHARLES: Yes, I did.
ANGELA: Are you feeling ok? You don't look well.

CHARLES: I'm just getting over a cold. We should go. Brian, can you bring my mother downstairs and have the doorman flag a cab?
BRIAN: Sure.
ANGELA: It's nice to see you again. I trust you've cleaned up that mouth.
BRIAN: Yes, I'm sorry about that.
ANGELA: Dennis, I'll leave the wig in the living room, and we can fix it later.
DENNIS: Ok.

(Brian and Angela leave.)

(Continued) Are you sure you feel up for dinner?
CHARLES: I have to. Just go, I'll be down in a minute.

(Charles sits on the bed and starts to cry.)

DENNIS: Are you crying?
CHARLES: No.

(Dennis starts to laugh.)

(Continued) Are you laughing at me?
DENNIS: I'm sorry but this is the first time I've never seen you cry.
CHARLES: I know. You're always the one crying.
DENNIS: Ouch. You're going to be fine.
CHARLES: I know.
DENNIS: I'll meet you downstairs.

(Music. Dennis exits. Charles is left sitting on the bed. During the scene change music Charles steps downstage into a single light special. The male nurse enters with an IV pole. He dresses Charles in a hospital gown and hooks him up to the IV bag. The actress playing Carol enters dressed as a nurse wearing a face mask [The male nurse does not wear a face mask.] She brings in a small chair and turns down the sheets on the bed. Charles gets into the bed and the nurse exits)

END OF SCENE

Act 2

Scene 3

(Charles is in bed he is attached to an IV. Dennis enters he is wearing a mask. He is carrying a gift and food to go container.)

CHARLES: You look ridiculous.
DENNIS: Thank you. *(He takes off his mask.)* They wouldn't let me come in unless I wore this. I tried to tell them that I'm not going to catch it by just being in here.
CHARLES: Well, for doctors they seem to be as scared as everyone else.
DENNIS: Where are your parents?
CHARLES: I sent them to out get something to eat. My mother was stressing me out. Every time the doctors' mention AIDS she tries to correct them which only causes a fight. My father just sits in the hallway. He doesn't really deal with things well.
DENNIS: Don't get yourself worked up. Did you eat today? I brought you some food from the memorial.
CHARLES: I can't I just get sick. *(Referring to IV.)* It's liquid lunch for me. Can you hand me that cup of water? *(Dennis does.)* How was the memorial?
DENNIS: It was beautiful, a little over the top. There had to be fifteen drag queens there. People were asking about you.
CHARLES: I really wanted to go.
DENNIS: They understood. *(Small pause.)* I saw Brian there.

CHARLES: Brian was at Edward's memorial?
DENNIS: Yeah, he said that even though Edward was mean to him all those years he still kind of cared about him. *(Small pause.)* He asked about you.
CHARLES: That's nice. Can we talk about something else?
DENNIS: Come on, he just wants to talk to you.
CHARLES: I don't want to talk to him.
DENNIS: Charles it wasn't your fault. He could have got it from anyone. No one can tell who they got it from.
CHARLES: He's a good kid. He doesn't deserve this.
DENNIS: It's not attacking bad people. They've even found some straight people who have it now.

(A male nurse walks in to change the IV.)

NURSE: You're supposed to be wearing your mask.
DENNIS: I'll be ok.
NURSE: That's what they all say. Can you just put it back on please?
CHARLES: How about you just change that damn bag and get the fuck out of here?
NURSE: I'm just doing my job.
DENNIS: It's ok Charles, I'll put it back on even though it makes no difference.
NURSE: I know that. I asked to work on this unit. Not a lot of people are anxious to take care of our kind.
DENNIS: I'm sorry.

NURSE: Just keep the mask on when the doctors and nurses are here.

(The Nurse starts to exit. He turns to Charles.)

(Continued) Mr. Elsen, can I ask you a question?

CHARLES: I'm hooked up to an IV pole and I can't leave this room, do I really have a choice?
NURSE: Is he always this irritating?
DENNIS: Welcome to my life.
NURSE: Mr. Elsen, can you please tell your mother to wear her mask when she's in here?

(Dennis and Charles look at each other for a second. They burst out laughing.)

CHARLES: And you think I'm irritating?
DENNIS: You have no idea what irritating is until you go toe to toe with his mother.
NURSE: Dear God, I need a drink.

(The Nurse exits. Dennis watches him leave.)

CHARLES: He's kind of cute.
DENNIS: Are you kidding me right now?
CHARLES: I'm not dead yet.

(Dennis changes the subject.)

DENNIS: I brought you a gift.

81

(Dennis hands Charles the gift. Charles starts to open it. He is having difficulty unwrapping it.)

CHARLES: You look good. Very healthy.
DENNIS: Thank you, I think.
CHARLES: Well, I mean I'm just stating a fact.
DENNIS: I don't know how many times I have to tell you that I'm not sick. I haven't tested positive.
CHARLES: I know it just scares me.
DENNIS: Scares you? You're the only person I know that is never scared.
CHARLES: They don't know how long I've had it. I could have had it for years and I just worry that I might have got you sick.
DENNIS: Charles we never slept together. You do remember that right?
CHARLES: I think I do. It's just these drugs they have me on make my brain all mixed up and make me all shaky. *(Referring to the gift.)* I can't even open this.
DENNIS: I'll do it. *(Slight pause.)* It was a bubble bath.
CHARLES: A bubble bath?
DENNIS: That's what we did. I saw you walking on the street in San Diego. I just walked out of a thrift store. I was carrying a box of Fiestaware.
CHARLES: Yes, I remember those awful colored cups.
DENNIS: Anyway, I saw you and we locked eyes. I got scared and I ran into a bookstore. You followed me and you turned on your charm. Next thing you know we were at my apartment in the bathtub.

CHARLES: That's right. I really hate these drugs. They make my head so foggy.
DENNIS: They're going to help you.

(Dennis pulls a pair of silk pajamas and a bathrobe out of the gift box.)

(Continued) Look at this.
CHARLES: They're beautiful.
DENNIS: It's silk. I know how you love to be comfortable. The robe is designer. I figured if you are going to be sitting in St Vincent's for a couple weeks you should look good.
CHARLES: I love them. I'll change into them later. How are things at the studio?
DENNIS: They're going good. I've hired a couple new people, just to help while you're out. I've found someone to take Edwards's spot. He's okay, not as funny but he might grow on me...us. I have to call Carol. She has a concert at Carnegie Hall, and she wants you to do her makeup.
CHARLES: And?
DENNIS: And I have to tell her you can't. She'll have to find someone else.
CHARLES: You can do it.
DENNIS: You're the makeup artist I can't do what you do.
CHARLES: Yes, you can. You've become an amazing makeup artist. When are you going to realize that?
DENNIS: No one can do her makeup like you can.
CHARLES: You can. I've seen you do it.

DENNIS: I can't.
CHARLES: You have to.
DENNIS: I'll hire someone to fill in until you come back.
CHARLES: What if I don't come back? *(Pause.)* What's going to happen to the company?
DENNIS: I don't know. You've never talked about it before.
CHARLES: I don't want it to end.
DENNIS: I won't let it, but you pay people out of your own back account. If something should happen, everything you have goes to your family and there's nothing any of us can do about it.
CHARLES: My mother can't run the company. *(With a little laugh.)* Can you imagine? There would be a whole division dedicated to styling her wigs.
DENNIS: What do you want me to do?
CHARLES: I don't know. Do I need to get a lawyer or something?
DENNIS: I can see what I can do, I'll call around and see if someone will come here and draw up a will for you. I heard of some lawyers working with people who are sick to make sure their final wishes are carried out. When people die their families are just coming in and taking everything. Edward's family came in, emptied his apartment, and didn't tell anyone. Nothing was left. It's like he never even existed.

(We hear Angela offstage yelling at the Nurse.)

ANGELA: No, I won't wear that mask. I'm fine, just mind your own business.
DENNIS: We'll talk about this later.
CHARLES: Ok.

(Angela enters.)

ANGELA: This hospital is awful. I wish you would just come home to get better.
CHARLES: I'm not going to come all the way home to go to the hospital. Manhattan is my home.
ANGELA: Dennis, how are you?
DENNIS: I'm good Angela, how are you?
ANGELA: I'm good, but can you please stop calling me Angela. I've known you long enough. You can call me Angie, my friends and family call me Angie.

(Dennis is taken back and surprised.)

DENNIS: Okay, Angie.
ANGELA: That's better. How are things at the studio going? Are you keeping things running smooth while Charles gets better?
DENNIS: Yes, things are great. We've hired some extra people now that we've lost Edward.
ANGELA: Yes, that was very sad. I always liked him.
CHARLES: Look, Dennis bought me pajamas and a bathrobe.
ANGELA: Well, look at those, fancy fancy.
DENNIS: I just want him to be comfortable.

ANGELA: I'll just hang them up in the closet for later.
DENNIS: I have to get back to the studio. I have some calls to make.
ANGELA: Don't get too comfortable playing boss. He will be up and around soon enough.
CHARLES: Mother stop it. Dennis, call me later and we can discuss what we talked about.
DENNIS: Ok. Get some rest. Goodbye Angela...Angie, if you need anything please call.
ANGELA: Thank you, I will.

(Music.)

END OF SCENE

A note about Edward's death. During both productions audience members expressed concern with Edward's death being very sudden and the character not showing any signs of being sick. This was done purposely to show what it was like in the early days of the AIDS Crisis. Many early accounts of the crisis were that people went from being visually healthy to sick and dying in a very short time. The audience should have no clue that Edward is sick in his last scene.

Act 2

Scene 4

(Charles is in his hospital bed. He is in a coma. Angela is in the room with him. Dennis is at the studio prepping to do Carol's makeup. Carol enters.)

CAROL: Dennis.
DENNIS: Carol. How are you? You look amazing.
CAROL: Thank you. I'm well. How are you?
DENNIS: I'm doing well. Shall we get started?

(Carol sits down and Dennis starts to do her makeup. The scene shifts to the hospital. The Male Nurse enters and goes to Charles' IV bag. He injects morphine into an IV port.)

ANGELA: What are you doing to him?
NURSE: It's just a little something to keep him comfortable.
ANGELA: He's in a coma, I thought he couldn't feel any pain.
NURSE: He can't but the doctor just wants to make sure.
ANGELA: How come you're not wearing a mask?
NURSE: What do you mean?
ANGELA: You argue with me about wearing a mask everyday but here you are not wearing one.
NURSE: Because unlike the rest of the doctors and nurses, I'm not afraid that I'll catch anything by being in here.

ANGELA: Neither am I.
NURSE: And a lot of my friends are sick
ANGELA: So, you've seen a lot of this then?
NURSE: Yes.
ANGELA: Do people come back from this?
NURSE: Not that I've seen. I can't imagine it will be long now.

(Scene shifts back to the studio. During the next lines between Dennis and Carol, Charles passes away. Light's slowly fade on the hospital scene.)

CAROL: I know it was so crazy, but as soon as Charles suggested that I throw that fit…I don't know, something just came over me.
DENNIS: I can't believe he talked you into doing that.
CAROL: I was young, and I was caught up in the excitement of the moment. I remember when I walked onstage that night, naked as the day I was born, I wanted to throw up. But that was the night that made me who I am today. A couple days later I got a telegram from Beverly Sills. *(She opens her purse and takes out the telegram.)* I keep it in my purse. *(She hands it to Dennis.)* Whenever I feel like throwing in the towel, I read it.
DENNIS: My darling Carol. Charles tells me you've arrived. Welcome to the club. Love Bubbles. *(They both laugh.)* Leave it to Charles. Everything he touches turns to gold.
CAROL: If anyone would know that it, would be you?

DENNIS: Well, it wasn't gold in the beginning. When Charles promised me this glamourous life in New York City it consisted of a one-bedroom studio with his ex-boyfriend and an internship with the Cincinnati Opera. I remember the day after we met he came back to my apartment just to make sure I was going to come back to Manhattan with him. By that point I got cold feet. As you know, Charles doesn't take no for an answer. So, he invited me to join him backstage at the San Diego Opera House. I watched him work and when the show started, he sat me offstage. I just watched awe. Charles created all these mythical creature makeup designs. The whole show was magic. I knew then that I couldn't say no. Then overnight Charles career took off and he took me along for a crazy ride. I sometimes feel like I'm living the life of a king.
CAROL: Don't you mean queen?
DENNNIS: That's a good one. *(They start laughing.)* I haven't laughed like that in a long time.
CAROL: Me neither. *(Small pause.)* It's so quiet in here
DENNIS: Well now that Edward is gone.
CAROL: I heard. That was so sad. I'm sorry.
DENNIS: It's ok. I miss him a lot. He always made me laugh.
CAROL: Where's Charles? I surprised he wasn't here to do my makeup.
DENNIS: I've been kind of running things for the past six months.
CAROL: What's wrong?
DENNIS: He's sick.
CAROL: It's not AIDS is it?

89

(Dennis doesn't respond. Carol realizes what she's saying is true.)

(Continued) Dennis, I'm sorry I didn't know.
DENNIS
He's at St. Vincent's. He's been in a coma for the past couple of days.
CAROL: You could have called and cancelled.
DENNIS: I couldn't. He wanted me to do this. *(His eyes well up.)* We just didn't expect it to go this fast.
CAROL: I hate this whole disease. Are you sick?
DENNIS: No, I'm fine. So…far. *(Handing her a mirror.)* Here, take a look. Make sure it's ok.
CAROL: Beautiful. Just like Charles. He taught you well.
DENNIS: Break a leg tonight Carol, I'm sure you'll be amazing.
CAROL: Thank you so much Dennis. Send my love to Charles' mother.
DENNIS: I will.

(Carol exits. The phone rings.)

(Continued) Elsen and Associates.
Angie…yes…are you ok? Yes…when? I'm sorry. I'm fine…do you want me to come to the hospital…? No, I guess it doesn't matter now…the apartment? That's fine I'll talk to you tomorrow.

(Dennis hangs up the phone. He goes to the makeup table, starts cleaning up the makeup and crumbles. He walks across the stage into the next scene.)

(No Music.)

END OF SCENE

Act 2

Scene 5

(Dennis looks around the room. There is an empty box on the floor. Dennis notices the coffee cup he gave to Charles in scene one. He picks up the cup, then sits on the edge of the bed, he sits for a moment and then takes the photo album out from under the mattress he sits and looks at the "man book." Angela enters with a box.)

ANGELA: What is that?

(Dennis quickly closes the photo album.)

DENNIS: Nothing, It's just my photo album.
ANGELA: Are you sure it's not Charles' album?
DENNIS: No, it's mine.
ANGELA: I just spoke with the landlord. He said you were planning on moving into Charles' apartment. *(Silence.)* You live next door. What's wrong with your place?
DENNIS: I like the view from these windows better. It's the best view in the building.

(Gets up to look out of the window, Angela watches Dennis for a moment.)

(Continued) It overlooks the Trinity Church Cemetery and the river. When the sun comes up its beautiful. Have you ever seen it?

ANGELA: Have I ever seen what?
DENNIS: The sunrise from these windows.
ANGELA: No. I don't think I would enjoy a view of a cemetery. I've seen enough death to last me a lifetime. *(Small silence.)* Besides I've never really spent that much time in here. *(Coldly.)* I suppose you have.
DENNIS: I was his best friend.
ANGELA: Well, I'm sure you're not the only "friend" who's seen that view.

(Beat. Angela puts the box she carried in on the bed.)

(Continued) Here this box won't fit on the truck. It's some of Charles' clothes. Roy doesn't really want them, and they won't fit you. Maybe some of Charles' other friends might want them.

(Angela starts to remove stuff from the shelves in Charles' room and packs them in a box. Dennis starts to go through the box.)

DENNIS: What are you going to do with all his other things?
ANGELA: I'm going to give them to his family. The antiques I'll sell. I know Charles and he would want to make sure I'm taken care of. *(Short silence)* Is there anything in your apartment I should know about?
DENNIS: Excuse me?
ANGELA: Is there anything in your apartment I should know about? Wigs perhaps?

DENNIS: Everything is at the studio. There are some wigs out in an opera right now but other than that they're all there. *(Short silence.)* I would never steal anything from Charles.
ANGELA: I had a dream last night, in the dream Charles came to me and said that there were wigs in your apartment.

(Angela stares at Dennis for a brief moment.)

DENNIS: I would never do that.

(Dennis finds the bathrobe he bought for Charles in the box of clothes, Dennis starts to cry.)

ANGELA: I'll take that as well.
DENNIS: I bought that for him.
ANGELA: I know.
DENNIS: What happened to the pajamas that go with the robe?
ANGELA: The black silk ones? I returned them. He never wore them. Besides, they won't fit you.
DENNIS: I wasn't going to wear them. I thought you might want to bury him in them, he liked to be comfortable.

(Angela changes to a stern tone.)

ANGELA: My son is not going to be buried in pajamas! I mailed his Tuxedo home to be cleaned.
DENNIS: It doesn't fit him.
ANGELA: I really don't think that matters anymore.

(Beat.)

DENNIS: Do you need me to do anything? He never really mentioned what he wanted if he ever died but I could help you plan if you want.
ANGELA: I've already called the funeral home. We have a family plot back home.

(Angela has picked up a framed picture of Charles off one of the shelves, she holds it in her hand as she speaks.)

(Continued) I haven't picked out a casket yet. If you want to do that you can. The service is next week, and I have a lot of things to sort out.
DENNIS: Ok. I can come into town a couple days early.

(Angela suddenly becomes emotional.)

ANGELA: The funeral home won't let me have an open casket. They won't even let me see him. How am I supposed to know he's going to be in the casket?
DENNIS: He had AIDS. They won't let anyone's family have an open casket. It's too dangerous…
ANGELA: My son did not have AIDS! He died of spinal meningitis!

(She throws the photo of Charles into the box of clothes on the bed.)

DENNIS: I know, but it was caused by AIDS.

ANGELA: It was not caused by AIDS, Charles told me he got it from feeding pigeons in Central Park.
DENNIS: He may have got it in Central Park, but it wasn't from feeding pigeons.
ANGELA: My son was a good man. He didn't have that disgusting disease.
DENNIS: It's not a disgusting disease. It's not a shameful way to die. People are sick all over the city. It doesn't make them bad people.
ANGELA: My son isn't like those people. *(Small pause.)* I suppose you're sick too.
DENNIS: I don't know, maybe we're all sick. This city is turning into a war zone.
ANGELA: Maybe if Charles just stayed away from this god forsaken place this wouldn't have happened.
DENNIS: It's not just happening here. It's everywhere.
ANGELA: Fine, but it doesn't matter to me. My only son is gone. I don't care what happens here anymore.

(Beat.)

(Continued) Do you have Charles' keys to the studio? I couldn't find them. I need to go and get the books.
DENNIS: Charles didn't have books. He paid people out of his own bank account.
ANGELA: I know that. I'm taking about the books with the contracts for the Opera companies. If I'm going to running things, I need to know who the contacts are.

DENNIS: What do you mean you're going to be running things? Charles had a will drawn up.
ANGELA: No, he didn't.
DENNIS: When he was in the hospital he asked me to get him a lawyer.
ANGELA: I know. I was there the day the lawyer came.
DENNIS: What did he say?
ANGELA: Nothing. I sent him away before he could say anything. Charles was too far gone. I wouldn't want him making any hasty decisions. *(Pause.)* Well, it looks like you work for me now.
DENNIS: No, I don't. Angie he wanted…
ANGELA: Please don't call me Angie.
DENNIS: You said I could.
ANGELA: My friends and family call me that. I'm your boss now.
DENNIS: Angela, he wanted me to take over the business.
ANGELA: Well, you can't. You can work for me, but my son wanted me to be taken care of.
DENNIS: I'm the one who's been running the company since he's been sick. I'm the one who knows all the contacts.
ANGELA: That doesn't mean anything to me. That company has Charles' name on it.
DENNIS: I'll walk and so will everyone else.
ANGELA: No, you won't. You wouldn't do that to him. You don't think I didn't know about Charles' feelings for you?

(There is no response from Dennis.)

(Continued) All those Christmas' you spent with us. I saw how he looked at you. He showered you with gifts. He spent more on you than he did on his entire family.
DENNIS: So, what? You're jealous.
ANGELA: I'm not jealous of anyone. What do I have to be jealous about? I got the company

(Dennis starts to plead with Angela.)

DENNIS: He wanted me…
ANGELA: No, he didn't! This is over. I will sort this out after the services. If you chose to stay with the company, we can discuss it then. I have to go plan my son's funeral. *(She starts to leave.)*
DENNIS: Do you still want me to pick out the casket?
ANGLEA: Do what you want.

(Angela leaves. As the music starts Dennis steps into the same special Charles stepped into during the hospital scene. He takes out an AZT prescription bottle and takes a pill. He is crying. He cries for Charles, Edward, and himself. The lights fade to black.)

END OF PLAY

*After Charles' death Elsen and Associates continued to design makeup and wigs for opera. They also designed the wigs for the Broadway productions of "Angels in America, part one and two," "Two Trains Running," "Jelly's Last Jam," "Caroline or Change" and "The Wild Party" starring Toni Collette and Eartha Kitt.

It is now run by Dennis and his husband. The company is no longer in New York City.

The cast of Chasing Charles – December 2014
(Pictured is Ann Milliken as Angela & Nathan Hoffman as Brian)

The cast of Chasing Charles – November 2015
(Pictured is Melissa Putterman-Hoffman as Angela

& Christopher Malatesta as Brian)

Oliver Ord as Edward, JJ Buechner as Dennis &
Ann Milliken as Angela

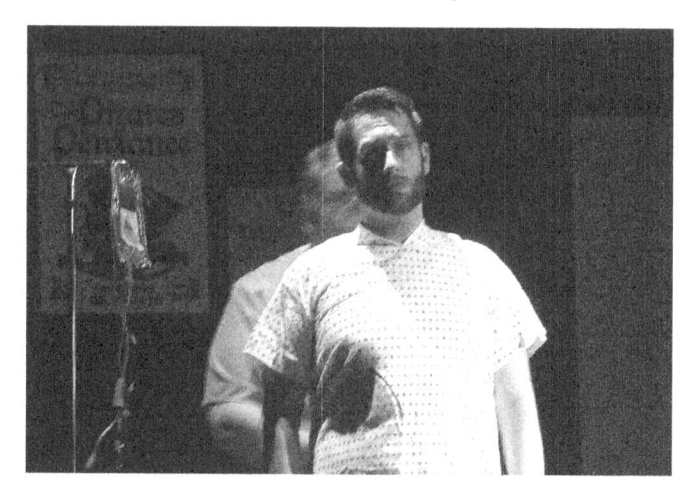

Matt DeMarco as Charles

Melissa Putterman-Hoffmann as Angela

Elizabeth Sterling as Carol

Roy, Angela & Charles Elsen

Roy & Angela Elsen

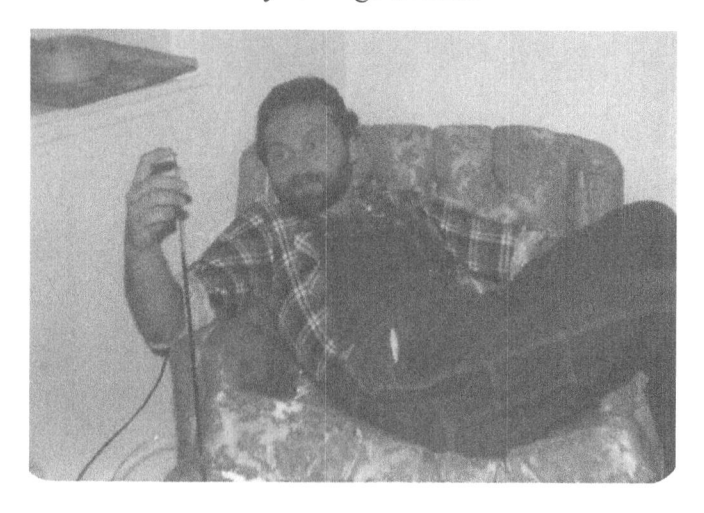

Charles Elsen